TELL ME HOW YOU ARE

A CHRONOLOGY OF LOVE AND LOSS

EDWARD PITTMAN

ISBN: 979-8-218-50841-8 TradePaperback
ISBN: 979-8-218-50840-1 eBook

DEDICATION

To those who inspired these poems, I owe you a debt greater than I can ever repay.

But most of all to Michelle. You are the last.

CONTENTS

In chronological order

MICHELLE

KARYN

THE BATTLE OF CHATTANOOGA

I have left behind a lover and a cat,

not a family who waits for word that never comes,

who, frowning, cringes at the sounds of shells

exploding in a town over the hill,

who watches the columns of smoke rise and merge,

darkening a sickly dawn.

I should have walked here.

No Honda's hum could hold for me

the same fear as those muddied footfalls.

No Perrier bottle approximates

the weight of a battered musket.

I hear the chirrup of a dozen or so sparrows

begging for my crackers,

not the whip-whip of Minnie balls

past my ears.

In the afternoon sun, I can see for miles.

No fog clings to these gentle slopes,

clouding the lens of my spyglass,

or dulls the glint of bayonets

approaching in the sallow light.

I hear a splash in the river,

the slap of horses' hooves in the mud,

feel the world drawing in its breath

in the last instant before the cannons fire.

Riding back to the motel,

my headache pounds like a wound,

and I imagine myself borne on a stretcher,

carried quickly past the dead and dying,

my fingers dragging the ground,

lifted gently by the hands of ghosts

into the future, into the light.

Two Stories

The deer drinks and shudders, but knows nothing.

Here by this stream, my tears fell, years ago,

and I am reminded of the story of a Bannock brave

— his bones lie here somewhere —

told to me in a bar in town,

a brave who came here to meet his lover.

He saw her on the other side of the water,

her back to him.

He heard the crunch of leaves behind him,

the snap of a twig under a heavy boot.

The last thing he heard was the boom of the .45-70.

In my dream, I am at the office.

I am doing geological things:

poring over porosity logs,

looking for the squiggles that will lead me to oil.

But the squiggles become the outline of a woman,

lying naked on a blanket, asleep.

I think I know who she is.

Then I notice I am almost naked,

wearing a necklace of bear teeth,

my loincloth askew.

I walk into the conference room,

but no one can see me, a lost man,

a man out of time.

The receptionist looks through me

to a salesman who has just arrived.

She walks through my outstretched arm,

and stops, her eyes wide, feeling something, then walks on.

I hear the crunch of leaves, the snap of a twig.

I reach for my knife but it isn't there.

There is the sound of thunder,

and the streets outside the building fill with rain.

I wake up in my sleeping bag,

my head filled with the fuzz of a dream

I will forget, little by little, for the rest of my life.

Throughout the night, the mist has been falling

from the mouth of a great bear with galaxies for eyes.

Outside the tent, I hear something moving:

the crunch of leaves, the snap of a twig.

I imagine it is the brave, retracing his steps,

wondering what went wrong,

asking himself the same questions

I have been asking myself for ten years now.

I was here once before, too, to meet a lover,

She waited for me on the other side of the stream,

her back to me, her hair black like the darkest space,

a vacuum for truth, love,

all swallowed up, decompressed, and torn apart.

This afternoon, I'll pack my things

and head back to Texas;

but now I sit here by the water,

watching two sad stories play themselves out over and over.

Once in a while, the eyes of the brave meet mine,

and there is an understanding:

Here we are blameless.

In this story we have done no wrong,

both of us ghosts returned to survey a landscape

we once thought we knew.

AMY

LAST CHANCE

Dear friend, dear congressman, one-eyed amigo,

soulmate in despair,

please lend me a cabbage or a once-used bandage

with the blood of a martyr in red pin dots there.

Autograph my cast, 'cause time's running out.

Confusions come like oily raindrops

and I'm running into the wind.

Oh compadre, oh housewife,

watching TV,

what I would do for a taste of that tangy blue stuff

before I have to go,

before they come to me at night and take me

to where there are no rotary engines,

no lizards, no red bees.

Hide me in a forest, hide me in a park,

you who work for the city,

playing basketball and eating free lunches.

Please leave me some chicken in that greasy, waxy tub.

The bones are the same as the meat.

Ma cheri, my partner,

can't we do-si-do,

and just let me wear those lederhosen one last time,

even though they're too small.

I think they'll fit me now.

And send me your pocketknife when I'm better,

and don't forget to take in my film,

and that noise the car used to make,

well,

the funniest thing:

It doesn't make it anymore.

KIMBERLY

MEMPHIS

My friend used to say

romances have to happen in Paris

and a goodbye doesn't have to be forever.

She was wrong, of course,

and I wonder how she took it when

all that wrong stared her in the face

that afternoon in September 1985.

Letters forever unanswered,

poems sent and returned unread.

On the telephone, her parents told me a story,

its ending still incomprehensible.

The leaves she collected,

the smiles she saved for quiet moments,

a dress she found by the roadside, sewed back together,

and wore first for me, only to take it off a moment later,

where are they now?

That day it was quiet in Iowa City,

the first breezes of fall tickling Amish cornfields,

and the wind washed her smell over me like

smoke from some forgotten campfire.

And on a road in Tennessee

the wail of the ambulance sounded its siren song,

calling a surprised soul to the world to come.

It was as if her belief in Memphis

could have changed everything:

rewritten the tarnished lives of factory workers,

soothed the throngs of tired waitresses

rushing along the dirty roads,

ushered in bright futures for battalions of lazy students

wondering where their days would take them,

scrubbed away years of disappointments

from the walls of buildings standing silent in the twilight.

The Memphis she imagined, I see

once in a long while on a television in a dream:

She's next to me on the couch,

telling me how Memphis will be different,

how it will reach out its warm southern hand

and take her in,

opening its doors to all its secret places.

On the television screen hundreds of people are cheering

as confetti rains from a sky stained the brightest blue

onto a girl in the back of a convertible,

waving to the crowd,

kicking up her heels as the wind whips around her tan legs

and raises oh so slightly the hem of a dress

repaired with crazy stitches.

And each time I turn my head to see her

missing from the couch

I think it's a shame she never made it.

M.

DREAMS OF NAKEDNESS

After Freud

In the dream, their faces will be indistinct.

They will not notice your condition.

When the officers approach,

you will be without your saber.

You will be unable to run.

They will look at you with solemn expressions.

Certainly this is significant.

On a train, bound for a fictional country,

you see a strange landscape from the window.

In the fields,

peasants work the soil with rusted implements.

They are naked in the rain, then in the snow.

You turn away as a bird cries out.

You watch it devour a worm from a kitchen window.

You are in your best suit,

and the house is filled with guests.

Then you are naked.

You make introductions,

trying to cover yourself, trying to escape,

but all the rooms are full.

In the last,

at the end of a long hallway,

a couple breaks an embrace.

He vanishes through the wall

and she turns toward you.

You raise your hands from your sex and step toward her

as she opens her mouth to speak.

The dreamer's embarrassment

and the spectator's indifference

represent a psychological contradiction,

and this distortion is rooted in wish-fulfillment.

So there you are, naked,

and she is naked, too.

Together you walk through the wall to the outside.

This is what you know about her:

Her tastes have changed.

She has discarded her old dresses

in favor of newer styles.

But her smile is still the same,

and still she rolls over in her sleep,

where she dreams she is in a tropical garden

without her blouse.

A Japanese man approaches her,

making a sweeping gesture with his arm.

"I made all this," he says, "years ago."

She looks into his eyes and sees a house full of people.

After a moment she finds you in the kitchen,

looking out a window, wearing nothing.

Dreams of nakedness are exhibition dreams,

and our desire to cover ourselves is a signal of repression,

a conflict of the will,

a clue to a secret that must and must not be displayed.

You smile as you observe a woman in the garden,

rising on a swing,

her hair stained the brightest gold by the afternoon sun,

which falls, impossibly fast, toward a far horizon.

You turn from the window and she is there.

You are not embarrassed in your nakedness.

DEAD BIRD

On my porch just now, I found a pile of feathers,

and in those feathers a deconstructed bird.

Its song had been removed, along with its throat,

and I sat there for awhile

looking into its one good eye.

It might have been the bird whose song

woke me yesterday morning while I dreamed about you.

Or it might have been a bird from your neighborhood,

blown astray by the storm now hovering over the Gulf,

who tried to find its way home and,

after a moment with my cat,

found itself winging its way through the silent skies

of the world to come.

There, in a land of a million, million trees,

it sings its simple song while it waits for us to arrive one day.

But now I sing to it my simple song,

its chorus about your uncertain smile,

its refrain the music of your laughter,

each note like the sound of a choir, almost murmuring,

deep, deep in my heart.

JOY AND REGRET

Regret is sitting in her room,

her head in her hands.

She rubs her eyes as she listens to the cries

of the Roman soldier whose sword pierced Jesus' side,

whose dreams plague him centuries after his death.

She hears the moans of the Spaniards who,

too late, realized all of the Aztecs were dead,

the markets and streets empty,

the temples filled only with the sound of wind.

Then the telephone rings.

It's Joy, and he's in a good mood, as usual.

"We're going on a picnic," he announces,

"so wipe your eyes and get dressed."

An hour later they're in a park,

eating strawberries as the sun inches toward the horizon.

"If only you'd gotten raspberries," begins Regret.

"Nonsense," says Joy, leaning over to plant an impromptu kiss

on Regret's juice-stained lips.

"I wish you hadn't done that," she chides, wiping her mouth,

"with all these people around."

But Joy is on the other side of the meadow,

waving his hands over a pair of lovers lying on a blanket.

They fall into each other's arms

and lose themselves in a kiss.

"Do you see them?" asks Joy,

appearing suddenly at Regret's side.

"They're so happy together."

Regret shakes her head.

"Actually," she says, "he misses the woman he almost married.

He got a job offer and moved across the country.

He thought she would follow,

but they drifted apart."

Joy frowns.

"And she feels guilty after sleeping with a friend of his

one night when they had all been drinking.

She thinks she should have told him then,

but knows that now it would ruin everything."

On the way home from the park, Joy is silent.

He's smiling, but his eyes are wrong.

Regret thinks about reaching over to hold his hand,

but does nothing.

Later, just past dusk,

she thinks maybe she'll call him to apologize –

for what she doesn't know –

but instead she stands by the sink,

scraping the skin from a carrot until

it's no more than an orange twig.

All night long, she wrings her hands,

while airliners crisscross the sky like lonely fish,

and sleepers turn and shiver as they lie dreamless,

and when the dawn comes at last she is still there,

the ashtray full, her cat wailing outside,

muttering two words like a mantra:

"If only. If only."

A Meeting

The eons and millennia seemed intractable.

The years were more sensible,

able to generate support among the weeks and days and,

on occasion,

to get a word in edgewise with the minutes.

But the seconds remained fractious as always,

flitting in and out of the session –

accountable, it seemed, to no one.

THE FACE OF SORROW

Still Kierkegaard believes the face of sorrow

must eventually reveal itself,

and many times he has been right,

but as he sits on his tiny stool staring up at the starless sky

the night refuses, after a thousand years,

to become the face of tragedy.

The people gather around him.

"Come on Søren," they plead.

"How long has it been since we've seen daylight?"

The philosopher will not budge.

"Change your shape," he says to the moon. "Show yourself!"

He waits for a sign,

for the age-old frown of a lost soul

to cross the beautiful silver orb

that rests in the sky like a lover's cradled head.

The moon is just as stubborn.

In his heart,

Kierkegaard knows he has been wrong this time.

In the end he gives up, goes back to his hut,

and starts peeling potatoes.

The cosmic machinery commences with a vengeance.

It is morning, then high noon, then evening,

the sun dipping behind mountains that turn

cool in the twilight, cold in the dark,

the valleys between populated by fireflies

filled with the sickness unto death,

winging their way in silence toward a lighted gap in a hillside

from which they will not return.

And Kierkegaard peels the same potato,

not looking down,

wondering about our need to penetrate

the façades that coat our vital lies:

I am beautiful.

When I am dead and gone they will all remember me.

These lies that form the skin of our shivering souls,

growing reluctantly in earth tainted by questions and doubt.

He wonders why the potato hasn't been peeled down to *nothing*.

Then he looks down and the thing is in his hand,

heavier and more pale than before,

carved like the face of a sad woman,

eyes heavy with sorrow,

lumpy tears rolling down wet potato cheeks

onto the floor beneath his trembling feet.

TRACEY

HOROSCOPE

In the morning, you cannot reconcile the tension of opposites.

Cling to your optimism, to your good fortune,

seldom remembered but as a gauze leftover from waking dreams,

a pall of confused illumination casting shadows over your luncheon,

where problem-solving Scorpio speaks to you softly,

patting your hand, in a language you cannot understand.

In the evening, the new moon gleams on an unfinished highway

where cars sit idling at the end of the concrete,

a broken, forgotten bridge become the edge of the world.

They face a screen where the Sun has joined Neptune at an excavation,

the earth-sign Capricorn gesturing into a pit

from which a bright light shines,

causing the Sun to shield his eyes

melting Neptune's shell, who crumples,

while Capricorn shakes his head, shakes his head,

and slowly fades away.

There is a rumble as the earth shifts, a signal the picture is over,

and from the horizon the ground opens,

the lights going up as the planet devours itself

and the chorus of car horns rises on a speculative breeze,

the saddest song you could ever hear.

I Used to Sing this Song

In the song, there was a girl

on a beach at sunset,

singing something about a man in a big coat

by a river covered with ice.

He was cold,

and the way he sang was like screaming,

and his song was about the fish under the ice,

swimming in the dark, thick water,

blind, sluggish, wanting to sleep,

and he was as cold as any man

in a song had ever been.

The girl in the song was singing

about this man as he looked up the beach

at some little crabs skittering across the sand.

The waves were rolling in,

and the man in her song

turned from the river and walked away,

his footprints buried after a while

by the snow, which had been

falling steadily for hours,

falling in the song,

falling in the head of the girl in the song

who was singing up the beach,

at the little crabs,

then out at the water where a fish jumped,

glittered, and she wondered where the river

in her song had been,

whether it lead to this sea,

whether the man in her song,

trapped in his winter,

could imagine water moving like this,

so fast, so much of it.

I forget how the rest of it went.

IN THE HEAVENS

I scan the heavens for you like a searchlight,

that I would suddenly come upon a flash of thigh,

the white of your belly,

and I would remain there, staring,

and not blink,

and hope that at dawn I would not find you

to be some trick of darkness,

bleached wood, scrap of shell,

some wrinkle of sheet

just enough like your shape

to reveal me for a fool.

TRACEY

Trembling fingers, trembling heart.

As your gay husband rubs your neck, your eyes roll back.

What is it they see while I watch television,

rewriting the episode,

comedy to tragedy,

Tim to Edward,

Melanie to Tracey,

an auditorium full of people

watching two characters

sitting on a bed in a dimly lit loft,

looking over each other's shoulders,

saying nothing.

The audience files out shaking their heads

as I cry myself to sleep.

In the dream,
a dime shines underwater,
Eisenhower half smiling
at a joke I have played upon myself
again and again.

Then your foot covers him up

and the ripples spread outward

toward the edge of the puddle,

are spreading even now

through this gray Brooklyn sky.

Why do you make love

when you're drunk?

Why does your vibrator

know your insides better than I?

Where is the place –

distant universe, cognitive loop –

where we are together,

and how best to get there

before the coming of another night?

But these are questions I do not ask you.

What is it I see deep in your eyes?

Fear of happiness.

Fear of intimacy.

Fear.

What would I take from you

that I would not return?

I remember things that never happened,

a love fashioned out of innuendo

and the trappings of tenderness.

And this is what I send into the universe,

what I tell the people who read my thoughts:

a beautiful lie I once wanted to believe.

KIMBERLEY

WHEN YOU WERE ALIVE

Who would have thought I would forget

the sound of your sighs,

and remember only the respirator's clicking hiss,

or that the dull thunder of your heartbeat

would be eclipsed by the monitor's untenable blip,

that I could forget the traceries of veins

just under your skin,

and remember only the lesions,

and the bruises makeup could not hide?

But I could never forget your laughter

or the way you danced sideways,

or the sad cakes you baked

in the middle of the night,

or the smile you had,

all the more precious for its brevity,

that you gave to me like a present,

when you were once alive.

REBEKKAH

AT THE FUNERAL

I helped carry the casket when David's father died.

There were rumors of his having once been a flamenco guitarist,

a great lover during his days in Chile.

I knew him only as an invalid,

staring through me from the bed,

cursing in halting Spanish,

his chest covered with soup.

During the memorial service,

a woman dressed in green sat on the other side of the aisle,

just behind the family.

During the second hymn, we caught each other's eye,

then looked away,

toward the frowning statues of saints long since dead.

When they wheeled the casket by, I broke down,

and no matter how hard I bit my lip I kept sniffling.

Across the aisle, the woman in green was sniffling, too,

and for a moment we were alike:

relieved to be crying, finally, for someone other than ourselves.

C.J.

THIS TIME

Each second of this strange relationship,

each Doppler-shifted instant falling

toward a history it cannot begin to imagine.

Every moment of our time together separate and distinct,

its own organism,

scarcely aware of the time through which it moves,

of the other moments brushing against it

like drowsy commuters huddled together on a speeding train.

Right now, the first touch of our lips on our first kiss

climbs into a taxi in Chicago in the early afternoon,

chats idly with the driver while considering its destination.

On the way to the airport it whistles a song,

slow and sad, that it will one day no longer remember.

The first time we made love –

the instant your eyes rolled back into your head

and a tiny tear began to inch its way across your cheek –

stares out across a quiet Montana lake just before dawn,

watching trout after trout leap into the chill air,

chasing mayflies that won't appear

for the better part of half a year.

And in a cargo plane circling high

in the night sky over a darkened continent,

a moment from our marriage yet to be

lies sleeping in a hammock,

its hair rustled by the wind swirling

through the open cabin.

It is the moment of the lifting of the veil,

that first glance into your changed eyes

filled with a promise they can scarcely bear.

Its eyelids twitch as it lies there,

clutching its parachute,

waiting for the crackly voice on the loudspeaker

to come one day,

perhaps years from now,

and tell it that it's time to jump.

It Didn't Last

Stain on the sheets,

stain on your soul,

the promise of these past three years ruined

by horrors that were never mine to remember.

What would I see reflected in the water

now pooling in your wide eyes?

We spoke different languages:

Me, the tumbling, clinging love

taught to me by my parents.

You, the maelstrom of grunts

and whimpers of shame

your uncle left you with

when he was finished.

In dreams I can talk to you.

We are from the same country,

seated at a desk,

writing with your hand on mine

the remembered story of our brief love

in words both of us can understand,

the most beautiful poem

we could ever hope to read.

RETURN

The desk clerk made his escape some time ago.

Where the windowpanes used to be,

hardy spiders crouch in thick webs,

swaying in the wind.

A rat's nest squats brazenly in the center of Room 7,

and the raccoons in Room 19 chitter like toy pianos.

There crows line the roofbeams –

a rotten ribcage soaked by the drizzle

from this November sky.

In the corner is the gouge in the wall

where your heel sank into the plaster

when I sank into you.

But that was some time ago,

and the wallpaper there is faded,

like the five faded summers

since I last whispered your name.

MARILYN

GHOST DANCE

I. The Indians

In the middle of the night

at the end of another forgettable week,

George Whispering Fawn Lee finishes the Ghost Dance.

As if by this combination of chants and movements

the Old Ones would return,

and the buffalo would fill the plains once more.

He's done it so many times

he dances it in his dreams.

Sometimes –

when the truck won't start,

when his wife gives him that exasperated look

she inherited from her mother –

the dance is all he can do,

and when he finishes, he goes into the house,

pats the dust from his legs,

and looks into the refrigerator,

for what he doesn't know.

Everything happens that night:

Somewhere, far off, some cosmic

machinery comes to life.

The Great Spirit stirs,

and with a wave of its hand

the stars shudder like ripples in a pond,

so quickly that even if you were watching

you wouldn't believe what you saw,

and in this world who can believe anything?

Sitting Bull appears suddenly, in mid yawn,

his wife beside him.

And Wovoka follows soon after, naked,

not that anyone notices.

Resplendent in his war paint,

Kicking Bear solidifies as if from mist.

After a time, there are thousands

of ancestors of ancestors,

staring up at the winter sky,

and the yips of the coyotes

herald their coming.

II. The White Men

This is where we leave the world.

One last kiss, your hands around my neck,

and we fade into air –

white shadows melted into nothing by a sullen sun.

There is the sound of thunder then,

and the buffalo – a brown sea – charge across the plain.

Rain in the Face and the others mount their horses

and notch their arrows.

Eyes glassy with tears, they begin the hunt.

After a time,

the lights in our apartment flicker, then are dark,

as a power plant whirrs slowly into silence.

Airplanes sit empty on runways,

and scratched flatware lies in soapy water

in restaurants across North America.

Cats and dogs run in the streets,

in the parks, in office buildings,

relieving themselves where they please.

We are no more than clouds,

hanging silent over a land that was never ours.

I pour my rain onto the plains of South Dakota,

and you sprinkle snow over a Wyoming meadow.

In time, this will be all we know.

We'll be much happier, you'll see.

STACIE

THIRTEEN LINES

The inscrutable smile in your profile picture,

the one that supposedly guards it all.

That crooked grin you've practiced

for the better part of 30 years.

Your quote,

lifted from someone else's quote,

lifted from a tombstone in a Cincinnati cemetery.

They didn't get it right,

but who reads Plato in the original Greek,

except the Greeks, right?

But the poem there on your page,

that is really something.

They used to write poems like that

before Plath stuck her head in an oven,

but rarely since.

Now, most of the time,

the device, the format, the conceit,

is more important than the words,

the thoughts behind the words,

and the truth winding like lost fog

among those thirteen lines you wrote, apparently,

in Sun Valley this past summer.

It is those lines that draw me back

at odd moments:

on Sunday afternoons when the *paletas* carts

ding, ding down the sidewalk,

on my rare days off work, just after lunch,

and at 3 a.m.,

when the vandals pass us by

because the monitor's blue glow

lights up the window in the study,

as well as the tears gleaming in my eyes.

YONNA

COUNTRY OF HOPE

There the moon shines all day,

and lovers hold hands —

tentatively at first,

then with a fervor we have seldom

maintained for very long.

There the sun shines all night,

browning the faces of children

who smile like we have not smiled in years.

We were not born here,

but we have been here before;

and after, when we opened our eyes

and found ourselves crying,

it was not because the dream had been so tragic,

but because of the world in which we awoke.

Sadness holds no sway in this country,

was exiled years ago,

sent shuffling along the street

that leads to the seashore,

pelted with stones and laughter.

And death is but an occasional guest,

come calling when someone

finally grows too weary to go on –

which is seldom,

because here the day to come

is always a fraction more sublime

than the day just passed.

Someday I would meet you here,

if only I knew the way,

could find in a dark drawer a faded map,

or hear the names of the streets that lead here

in the notes of some sweet birdsong:

in the coo of sleeping doves

or the early morning rant

of some petulant warbler

who wishes us only joy,

and by some trick of circumstance

or accident of scope

we would find ourselves among the cheerful souls

in this bright country of hope.

DANA

ABOVE THE LABYRINTH

I watch all this from on high,

forgetting there are those higher still.

Below, spread out for years,

each brick each shrub

lies coated with dew like industrious ants

frozen by a death they could not have foreseen.

In the center of the maze,

my mother turns in ten-hour circles,

teaching English to the Chinese students

who follow her as she feels her way

among the towers of holly.

To the west,

nearly on the horizon,

David punches the bricks with bloody fists,

as if to make his own way,

one of several exits unseen only a few feet behind him.

Three hills away,

at the entrance to the nest of briars,

Christy and Tracey sit cross-legged on the lawn,

destroying and reassembling a single daffodil.

Dawn comes and goes like the touch of an uncertain lover,

and still I stand there above the labyrinth,

my feet asleep, my legs aching.

I do not know what else to do.

My brother walks his path too fast,

makes many wrong turns,

and my sister moves too slowly,

when she moves at all.

For months she stands at the rose archway,

unable to choose between the sandy path

and the rainforest trail.

Slightly north,

underneath a warmless winter sun,

my father picks his way among columns of ice.

In them he studies salmon frozen in mid leap,

the shadowy beak of a penguin,

the single blue-green eye of a coelacanth,

trapped millions of years from its home.

Yonna follows the stream

dividing the labyrinth

into day and night,

her right arm browned by the sun,

her left arm glowing in starlight.

She follows the curves of the stream

as it traces the curve of the world,

and with a wave the gates of the maze

open like flowers in bloom.

Then below me I see you,

seated on a bench in the field of marigolds,

the animals of the labyrinth

rolling about your feet like laughing children.

Above your head,

the book of poems you have yet to write

hangs like an overripe apple

in a tree stained with the colors of an early fall.

I climb down into the maze

and am instantly lost.

The paths I swore I would remember

fade like a favorite dream.

But still I feel my way among the thorns,

advancing and retreating,

pausing to stare at the sky

as if the shifting clouds could steer me

through this uncertain land,

looking always for the silent sign —

blink of firefly, tumbling leaf —

that will lead me, finally, to you.

FATE

The streets thrum with the leftover motion of the day,

and junebugs thump against my legs

like chores I meant to forget.

Here in the dark on the front porch

I make promises to you

I am not allowed to keep,

recite half remembered monologues

from a love story as yet unwritten,

dream of kisses that last until the dawn

whispers across the tops of my feet.

Like the light from a glass of milk

that calls to me when the stars have gone to sleep,

when all the declarations of the day to come

rest on dreamers' lips like the feathers of angels,

is that intangible moment where we stand nose to nose,

each of us helpless but to kiss the other.

In a future I am unable to see,

the fates place your hand on mine

and entwine our fingers like some slowly woven tapestry,

point our car to some unknown destination,

and with a sad smile turn away from a life

they would make their own,

if only they could make themselves believe.

DANCING

A cassette I won't remove from the tape deck,

frozen between *My Prayer* and *Since I Don't Have You,*

the steps between the kitchen and the table where you sat,

and the steps to the kitchen again.

From somewhere far off, I hear a song carried on the breeze,

its tune almost familiar,

and I wonder if you will someday hear it, too.

Commandeering merry-go-rounds throughout childhood,

kissing my pillow in the hours before dawn,

falling, dizzy, into a pile of leaves one cool Montana autumn,

walking with eyes closed to the bedroom of a lover,

wondering if I can remember the way.

All my life I have practiced for these slow turns I make with you.

The world is spinning, spinning,

as we walk past each other's offices.

And the moon rises and sets

as we raise our glasses in some darkened bar.

And the stars creep across the sky

as we turn over in our sleep.

Ours is a dance no teacher could teach,

and the diagram telling me where to move and when

is painted on a curtain behind which you stand,

dressed in a gown from a dream you cannot remember.

Now the orchestra is silent,

and now I lean against the wall and wait for your entrance,

knowing my heart will catch in my throat

when the music rises and I reach for your hand.

TIME TRAVEL

I do not want this moment to end.

In this moment my uncertainty about you is certain.

The sky at five a.m. is still dark,

but for airplanes high in the night clouds

carrying passengers away from and back into

the arms of sleeping lovers.

Somewhere, a man is sweeping up the shattered bar glasses,

and somewhere a dog is kicking his legs in his sleep,

chasing a cat he will chase for the rest of his life, but never catch.

And a car crawls slowly through the gravel of a road's shoulder,

nursing a thumping flat tire.

And in a neighborhood she doesn't recognize,

a young girl feels the clouds of an unknown drug part in her head

and looks up at a single star, light years away,

its light seemingly impossibly bright.

What are you thinking as you lie sleeping,

dreaming perhaps of a life that may someday be your own,

or a life separated from this existence by a path you chose

as a child on an afternoon you've since forgotten?

I warm up the equipment as I prepare for my jump:

tape recorder, pen, airline ticket,

dog-eared map to a place I've never been,

and the smell of your perfume,

which enshrouds me like some strange armor.

And I leap into a future where I hope to find you,

adrift on a fool's errand I want to last a lifetime.

SIX

You are the water

that holds me under.

You, the counterclockwise

turns I make in my sleep,

rolling over

six times each night.

Six times? you ask.

Not many.

But think of six miles

of frozen farmland,

six miles of winter river

under an inch of ice.

CAVE

Inside a cave,

buried under centuries of permafrost,

scrawled on stone by a hurried hand:

the recipes for stars,

the equations for constructing a universe,

the spells for making a love our world may never know.

RORSCHACH

This image is not open to interpretation.

The plate in question seems clear to some:

twin buffaloes, locking horns, stretched tall.

But who of us could not see a woman's face

bent to a mirror.

What some thought were buffalo legs,

clearly are the tracks of tears.

And this one – glob with bat wings –

your face in rain,

smeared by the windshield wipers

whipping the light and shadow

like a drunk whipping a dog.

This wide line here,

your mouth, lips parted,

saying something beautiful I'm sure,

or perhaps singing the first line of a song

I hope one day to hear.

And this plate here,

seemingly impossibly complex.

Here you hold the camera,

squinting at some far-off subject,

and here you are hunched over your diary

(I cannot read the words),

and here you are surrounded by flowers,

asleep in a field that looks somehow familiar.

But here, near this corner,

you stand on a hillside,

whispering sweet nothings to the clear,

unanswering stars.

It is in this plate I look for myself –

some scratch of the pen, blurred ink smear –

hoping someday to be surprised

by the sight of my presence

at your side.

IN YOUR CITY

The light of afternoon stains the streets

as my car nudges the curb.

In a clothing shop, the salesclerk clutches a pair of vinyl pants.

She taps her foot and sucks idly at her finger.

In a restaurant across the street,

couples hold hands and whisper secrets to one another,

shared confidences that seem so important now,

but that one day will be forgotten.

Behind a storefront window, a couple seems to sway

to music only they can hear,

but when I approach the glass I can see they are not moving.

Their chins nestle into each others' shoulders,

and their eyelashes rest against their cheeks.

They are sound asleep.

A billboard glows in the sky over a factory to the east.

On it is a single word: Love or loss.

From here it is impossible to tell

as the fog rolls in, obscuring nearly everything.

I wonder if I should be here,

in this city of lights and whispers,

of sighs and broken promises and hope.

In a hospital room, a women grimaces,

and a baby's cry echoes in the hallway as it is taken away,

while across town a man cradles his face in his hands,

pondering the enormity of a mistake he only now begins to realize.

In the houses, husbands and wives play hide and seek.

When they find one another they are surprised,

and they share a look they haven't shared in years

before falling into each other's arms.

And in the dark avenues, lovers gasp

at that first, almost unexpected plunge,

and the wetness on their skin shines in the light of the moon.

I walk these streets all night,

my lips wet from rain falling from invisible clouds,

or perhaps from even higher,

from the silent stars.

Just before dawn I realize I have no money,

and I begin the long walk back to my car.

But I know I will return

when I smell your perfume long after you've left,

when you cock your head just so

and the look in your eyes turns my tongue to stone,

when I see you walking away, and I am helpless but to follow.

I CANNOT GO FAR

I cannot go far.

My soul returns to you

like geese return each spring.

Before I kissed you

my heart was mired in winter,

but now I am warmed

by your hands on me,

your mouth against my chest,

your sweet weight atop me

while you move, eyes closed,

lost in your unfathomable thoughts.

TRAVELING

In the morning, I remember a newspaper story

about a region in the Amazon,

a place where the jungle seems impenetrable.

It is hard to see you as we worm our way past wet ferns,

over a carpet of cool moss,

through a shallow stream nearly a mile wide

that tugs at our ankles

like the insistent hands of children we never had.

When you turn to face me,

I am blinded by the light in your eyes.

At noon, an avalanche thunders past our mountain cabin,

and my passion comes on suddenly as an alpine storm.

Afterwards, you whisper to me words I will hear

in every dream for the rest of my life,

and your breath hangs in the air about your face like fog.

In the afternoon, we sit on a train,

riding, silent, through some unnamable country,

conjuring sad moments for ourselves

from marriages that no longer exist.

We lean together and fall asleep,

and I awake to the touch of your hair on my lips,

twitching in the air of the cabin like butterfly wings.

Later, I imagine a Mexican plain,

and a reed-roofed country house with an audience of dark desert,

and beaded lizards slumbering in the light of the moon.

And this is where we spend our evenings,

our laughter echoing over the silent sand,

walking about in the yard with rake and walking stick,

slowly shaping our story with careless hands.

In the middle of the night,

the reindeer creep up to the edge of our tent.

They snort in the cold,

rubbing nose to nose while you roll over

in your sleeping bag,

your flushed cheeks bathed by the glow

of the Northern Lights.

I watch you all night like this,

praying the morning never comes to steal you away.

THANKSGIVING

Cars whirr along the new roads,

fires roar in hearths,

and prayers of thanks wend their way toward heaven

like sparks from a signal fire

broadcasting an unbelievable message.

At night, the sounds of America frightened Pilgrims

huddled under blankets woven half a world away.

They tilled the soil of this strange land,

befriending a people they could not understand.

You sit across the table.

With my painted face, I feel suddenly absurd.

The feathers of my headdress flutter in the breeze,

as if they would fly to you.

I scarcely taste the food,

sitting there with a people I do not know,

conscious my people are losing their grip on this time.

One by one they slip into the past,

and then I am alone,

and I look across the table to see you still there,

a look in your eyes that may be real or imagined.

What is the language you speak?

What are the stories of your life?

What music is it that pours from your lips

like the song of a dark bird come to steal me away?

In my heart, I have no country.

I am lost in your wilderness,

living with the daydreams of gestures

you have yet to make.

On the road to Houston, my spirit animal

runs through the woods beside you,

its scales still warm from a sun

that set in Plymouth nearly 400 years ago.

What beings fashioned you from stardust

and the dreams I could not carry into the light of day?

Each day you keep the spirits' hands so busy,

as they remake you hour after hour.

In the afternoon, when the air is still,

I walk here, but only in the shadows,

lest the camera of a tourist

capture the ghost of my soul.

I wander through the fog that rolls in with dusk's half-light,

looking for a flash of your slip,

for the shadow of your hair cast on birch bark.

From the stars, the space between us seems infinitesimal.

From the shoulder of the Great Bear

I would swoop down to you like a hawk,

carry you over forests lit by fireflies,

over oceans where fish lumber fathoms deep,

to a place I cannot name.

I put down my lance to take up your hand,

dead these past few years,

to which your blood has now returned,

feeling a tingle I hope to feel for the rest of my life.

At sunset, I have seen the blush in your cheeks.

At midnight, the moon glows with the white of your smile.

And each morning I wake with your light in my eyes.

ARCHAEOLOGY AND PALEONTOLOGY

I sing songs from a cold sea, wordless chanteys from a time

before there were ships or men to sail them,

laments filled with the rumble of volcanoes in the night,

of the grind of glaciers the size of continents

creeping past herds of ice-bound moose.

Who will scoop out this sea

and lay it in some nearby depression?

What breath will dry this earth to prepare it for my coming?

Pickax and notebook,

brush and compass,

twine and wooden stakes,

I'll divide this dead land into grids,

each subdivision its own infinity.

As the sun sets, I'll chip away crumbs of earth

from the fossils of lives almost recognizable,

extract the winter from beetles

immobile in an amber dawn.

Far underground, a river lumbers

past the absurd tail of Ankylosaurus,

past tiny trilobites encased in limestone,

past legions of gastropods stopped in time by a winter

without a spring,

past your eyes as you lie in the grass,

watching the geese fly south

like bombers on their way to Armageddon.

I peel the quaternary period from the tertiary

like a child peering into his mother's jewelry box,

pry the delicate husks of spiriferoids from the shale,

their spiral shells staircases to mute prehistory,

stare in wonder at microfossils of pollen

sprung from the stamens of flowers dead for millennia.

A plane slides silent through the sky overhead.

How many of the passengers can feel you here?

Perhaps only a child,

nose pressed to the window,

watching his destiny written in the shifting clouds,

his failures and triumphs performed by warriors and maidens

of water vapor painted on a heavenly hieroglyph

that will not see tomorrow's dawn.

Your death would make tombmakers weep.

How many soldiers and horsemen to guard your lips

from the reaper's scalpels?

How much gold to capture the swell of your breasts,

the curve of your hips?

What jewel-encrusted sarcophagus could contain your lost light?

I carry the skeleton of the future

I've been assembling for thirty-three years,

lay it piece by piece softly on the dirty canvas,

turning the bones over in my mouth like rice noodles,

my tongue coated with the bitter, dusty taste of what might have
been.

Now the museum is closed,

dark but for the occasional trails of light

from the flashlights of thieves.

In what dark storage room is there space

for this boxful of the insignificant?

Someday, some sleepy archaeologist will lay us upon a table –

my fossilized patella nestled against your splintered clavicle –

and guided by picture books, arcane knowledge, and intuition

will piece together our past with patient hands.

Were we friends or lovers or something more?

Tonight, I sleep the sleep of the dead.

I walk barefoot past the mumbling Sphinx scratching at its flank,

past unshaven prophets huddled in doorways

pondering martyrdoms they cannot remember,

past hollow-eyed archangels polishing their swords,

and demigods rewriting the legends

those who once worshipped them have long since forgotten.

When I find your tomb, it is still sealed,

and I sit down in the dirt,

whiling away the eons conjuring ants and sowbugs,

waiting for the sound of stone grating on stone

and the touch of your hand on my shoulder,

an impossible answer to a question I have always longed to ask.

What I Cannot Forget

The hesitant touch of your lips

draws me back again and again,

like the wings of a hundred butterflies.

I close your eyes with kisses

and open them with my sighs.

My hands cup your breasts,

reading the braille of your passion,

and in the middle of the night my mouth finds your nipple,

the answer to a question my heart posed some time ago.

Later, I wake to feel your sleeping breath warming my chest,

where the hairs wave like stalks of grain ripe for harvest.

Between your legs is a mystery I hope never to fathom,

a taste plucked from paradise,

delivered by errant angels.

Your smile was stolen from myth,

from stories too beautiful to be read by mortals.

But still my eyes pore over your pages,

each hair, each curve, committed to fallible memory,

and each blink of my eye sends a prayer

I will see you like this all the days of my life.

Your shoulders are the hills of some unnamable country,

covered by an early snow,

lit by the light of exploding stars.

I would follow them all night,

while my feet froze,

while the wind turned my mouth to stone,

to the door of some mountain cabin

where I would find you naked before a dying fire,

a look in your eyes I have long dreamt of seeing.

The curve of your hips under my hands,

the ripple of goosebumps as my fingertips stroke you.

This is what I feel in my hands when I close my eyes.

I would cover you like a wave no moon could pull away,

feed you the taste that is mine alone,

then pause to taste it on your shining lips.

The wine has gone to our heads,

and our clothes fall from us like leaves

before I take you on the couch.

For a time, we are one body with two heads,

a wet machine between our legs

pounding out the rhythms in our hearts.

You follow me to the bedroom like a tiger.

On an arid plain I turn to face you,

show you my belly,

and close my eyes to wait for your claws.

With your taste in my mouth,

I give impassioned speeches on the road to the office,

and with the evidence of our lovemaking

coating me like translucent armor,

I wend my way through a weary world.

Our spring will never end.

Instead, death will make us shadows

drawn into one another by the moonlight

strained through trees in autumn,

by sun browning the arms of husbands and wives,

by firelight reflected in the eyes of lovers yet to be.

In a dream, I am in a church.

There is no one there.

I follow the sound of a fugue to the sanctuary,

and find you kneeling at the altar,

wearing only a bridal veil of sunlight.

This is where I would spend the rest of my days,

while the world rushes by,

and presidents enter and leave hospitals,

and abandoned spouses sit with their heads in their hands,

and infants cry because they know the future,

and all the while history makes its scribbled notes.

The world turns through space as you turn away from me,

and a volcano rises from a steaming sea

as you raise your hips for me,

and I push into you like I have done so many times

in daydreams these past six years,

like I push into you in a future

I am only just now beginning to imagine.

It is late, long after midnight,

and my cat laps at the dishes in the sink

while I lap at that place between your legs.

In the glow from the candles, you are a desert

lit by the signal fires of nomads,

your stomach a plain to be crossed after a lifetime of preparation,

your breasts hills of cream leading to heaven,

your mouth open, lips moistened by your tongue,

whispering words I cannot hear

as your thighs press against my ears.

I would cling to you in this place out of time,

where our twin heartbeats deafen death,

where your stomach warms my ear

and my hands brush across you like a breeze

from some forgotten place,

where our eyes watch one another's in dawn's half-light,

and drop, demure, like flocks of birds in flight.

WATCHING

What gray colossus watches over you,

frowns at the distracted suitors

who paint your future with fickle plans?

What towering golemn

will swat away your disappointments,

carry you in his palm like a frightened ant

to some safe place?

My hands are small,

but I carry what I can:

stammered condolence,

murmured prayer,

trying always to hide my surprise

when you do not turn away.

YOU

You are a love letter slipped under my door by God.

You are his handle on the world.

When he sees you after a day

of watching the world he made,

does he wonder at what unforeseen miracle

placed you here?

Does he marvel at chance, pause,

and look over his shoulder for something

greater even than he, perhaps, at work?

Does he shed a surprised tear at this happy accident,

which he brushes away, quickly,

before anyone can see?

SEEING

A few streets away, dogs howl in peculiar harmony.

Carried on the wind, their cries sound like your name.

The past knocks at the door to the present,

which, hypnotized, casts spells it receives from leap years

into a future more certain than any of us would like to believe.

In the yard, I still the leaves to divine our fate.

The orange oak leaves snake across the sidewalk

like the arm I would wrap around you in sleep.

The leaves fallen from maples months ago,

turned to veiny skeletons, flutter like your eyelids did

when I last recited to you the secrets of my heart

like some embarrassing confession.

And just before I am able to see the moment where our love

is decided for us,

the wind scatters them all into the street,

where the wheels of some dark car grind them suddenly to dust.

SLEET

I remember every word you said,

biting my lip while I watched the rain on the windshield

blot out the world drop by drop.

I walked to the party with the legs of a man condemned.

With the hands of a synchophant, I offered you a glass of wine.

And with the tongue of an alcoholic preacher,

I told you everything but what I wanted to say.

There is a part of me that withers away,

while later another part of me stumbles over my corpse, still warm.

Later still, illuminated by a single candle,

I perform an augury on myself,

mapping in my scattered entrails the road leading, finally, to you.

Later still, as the investigator, I sit you in a chair,

and in the light of a campfire fan out before you

dozens of photographs from a love that might have endured.

I seem to see a single tear perched just behind your eyes,

but in this uncertain light it is impossible to tell,

and I leave you there with the specters of your future lovers

to sip my coffee, already cold.

Now the sleet is falling from a dark sky.

I stand outside in my bathrobe

while a stray dog sniffs my leg,

hungry for something it cannot define,

and hour after hour I watch the roads become impassable

until finally I turn away.

WHAT I MUST DO

Whereas before she was enigmatic –

woman of a hundred nightgowns,

all delicate as butterfly wings –

now she is bored.

The clothes are the same,

to be sure,

but now when she stares out the window

she bites her lip and does not smile.

The mountains have been similarly afflicted.

The sun casts no gleam on the snow,

which seems dull,

more gray than white.

And the carpet of pine needles

still smells the same,

but I can't help thinking that someone

needs to get in here with a rake and clean up a bit.

I remember when it all used to mean something:

when making love with you was like a slow spell,

whispered to us by angels.

Now it's just meat on meat,

and your taste,

once so like chrysanthemums and coriander,

is mucous and nothing more.

I sold our magic to beggars to light their fires,

and the passion we once had, I sprinkled

on sleeping wolves (who truly mate for life)

one winter just outside Cody.

I do what I must:

take different roads home,

sleep with the lights on,

watching through the blinds for a belief

I am careful to keep just outside the door.

WHAT I KEEP

Flying over this brackish sea

I am Noah's dove,

searching for the scraps of broken promises,

the soggy reeds from an abandoned nest,

the remembered dreams of fervent whispers

fading from this drowned land.

The flutter of my wings

a white flash against

the afterimages left by lightning –

lips here, forming forgotten words,

an eye there, with tear –

bisected by angry clouds.

Banking now over a thousand lakes

washed into one another

like the lives of acquaintances.

I let go of all else.

One thing I take back with me,

homing in on a stripe of warmth

tangled by the cold, wet wind.

Flying away, he was a small man,

as he threw me into the air

like a gift into the hands of a stranger.

Now that I've returned, he's smaller still.

He limps across the deck of the ship,

its planks swollen with something

he cannot understand.

I will not give it up:

this shred of dress

from a life no longer my own,

this torn good-bye that keeps turning me always

in and out of love.

WATCH

In the heat of high noon, love comes apart like a cheap watch.

The tiny spring of our hand-holding

tumbles across the table to rest against a book unread for months,

and the way I look into your eyes

is revealed to be nothing more than a small metal bar,

scarcely wider than a hair,

that in this damp air has already begun to rust.

But later, when the fire in the hearth has died,

and later still, when the cats have gone to sleep

and their night souls traveled to the place

from which all cats have come,

the watch sits on the table,

its foretoken of our love's fate only half complete,

when from its tin guts comes music that, alas,

only a child could hear.

JULIA

YOUR TRAIN

Trains you see in dreams:

black, that roar in the night –

thunder on rails.

Or trains at noon:

silent as clouds,

as the whispers of lovers in memory.

You thought the dream was nondescript:

a picnic in some fog-shrouded meadow

with a handsome, gentle man,

the kind of man who has so often escaped you.

Then you see the train,

and although your mouth is open,

what you would have said to this man

you now know you will never say.

You get up from the blanket

and walk toward the tracks,

leaving him behind.

The strawberry he holds

he will always hold,

and he sits on the blanket

waiting for you to return.

He is sitting there even now.

When you reach the tracks,

the train is moving impossibly fast,

its cars a blur,

and in between each of them

you see, like twitches in time,

your first kiss,

your face when you knew you would

leave your first husband,

the last canvas you will ever paint.

Then you are on the train,

standing on the ledge between two cars

while the gravel rushes past underneath you,

and the wooden ties flash by like the sun strained through trees,

shining through the windshield on your hand

on the steering wheel that time you were in love.

When the train reaches the platform

you step onto the planks.

The ticketmaster grins and tips his hat.

The conductor checks his watch,

regards you sternly.

I am only a baggage boy

with a peculiar way of speaking

that I let some believe is second sight,

and although your bags are heavy,

I step forward just the same.

LEAVES

The leaves on the cooling sidewalk map out sadness –

quick pictures of destruction.

Tumbling so quickly, they are hard to see,

but the eyes in my heart are quick

when it comes to tragedy.

Two Ships

It is that time of day

when the light is suddenly strange.

The color is always different

but the feeling is the same:

something missing, missing from you,

that you didn't realize was ever gone.

Out on the water, the sea draws away,

vanishing down invisible drains,

and the ships sit tall in the sand

like weather vanes.

I can see your ship,

mired just beyond the breakwater, in open sea.

I abandon my ship

and start off across the bottom,

breathing the salt air where jellyfish once swam

like tiny, magic cities.

It will take me years to reach you.

Lunches of raw fish, dead for many months,

mouthfuls of mud littered with the bones of what once was,

but I start out just the same,

leaning into a sea wind that blows still,

dragging my nets behind me.

A LITTLE HOUSE

Driving one night, very late,

down the long road that led to your home

(although mine was much farther still),

we saw, down a narrow gravel drive

you had not seen before,

a small house revealed by moonlight.

You rolled down the window so quickly.

"To see it better," you said.

I pretended not to see you biting your lip,

and the wind took your tears so quickly that,

even now, I cannot be sure they were there at all.

We could have lived there.

If I had taken that turn, we would have arrived

to find the house empty of others' lives,

and would have filled it with our own.

Some night, when autumn turns to winter,

when my shame is but a shadow

of what I feel when I think of you,

I will meet you there.

Standing naked by the fire, you will think me a lost god,

settled in this place by some trick of destiny,

like you once thought of me

in the year before you knew me so well.

IN MY NEXT LIFE

In the moment after death,

regrets will gnaw at my soul like termites.

In my next life, I will not work so much.

I will pull my car to the side of the road to watch the sunset.

I will walk outside in winter, stand in the snow,

listen to the sound of my teeth chattering.

I will pray more for others.

I will step lightly on fallen leaves and fallen men.

In my next life, I will not know you.

I will live, content, on the side of a hill

in some oak-shaded wilderness.

I will marry a simple girl from a nearby town,

and we will set about the business

of love and raising children.

But when I dream, I will remember you.

Your eyes will be like twin moons

over the city where we met.

By then you will be gone,

but I will wander those streets like a ghost,

searching for evidence of your passing,

waking always with a sadness I cannot explain.

Michelle

PARADE

The parade comes at dusk,

egressed from buildings where

dreams die quarter by quarter.

Small promise made to a community on the wane,

the marching band plays its song,

garbled karaoke rant serenading an audience of dust.

Floats lumber by, faded skins littered with patches,

sad sharks creeping twilit streets.

Shuffling, somnambulant,

come sad-eyed elephants,

trunks swaying in the lagging breeze.

One turns its head and nods.

Twitch of an eye or knowing hierophant wink, who can say?

A gaggle of twirlers, failed starlets all.

Costumes stained with sweat and disappointment

twinkle in the half-light like winter stars.

Ragged ponytail, spinning your batons like pinwheels,

moonlight gleaming off a rust-flecked tiara,

you wear your borrowed uniform as best you can.

The baton clanks against the pavement,

and you scoop it up as the parade rolls on.

Broom blisters haunt my hands,

dirt in palm lines tracing maps to nowhere.

I step forward as a cup twirls,

crumpled ballerina, toward your feet,

and you step from the line,

smiling the only smile you've ever had.

The drum major raises his arms and stands patient,

as we look into each others' eyes for a minute,

then a decade, then a lifetime.

Then he waves his mace and the procession lurches on,

knowing I was destined to cross your path,

just as you were destined to pause.

Your hand is cool in mine,

but it will warm, in time.

Until I Met You

Until I met you, I had forgotten the sky,

that I could fall into it on a summer day.

I had forgotten sleeping in the sun,

and waking from dreams with tears

in my eyes I could not explain.

I had forgotten prayers,

and how happy it made me

to pray for others.

And I had forgotten how it felt

to kiss a lover for the first time.

Help me to remember that now.

ON THE CUSP OF SUMMER

Here, on the cusp of summer,

after deaths and disappointments

and misremembered rememberings.

After love letters, now yellowed, to lost lovers

and empty afternoons, and mornings,

waking alone, happy, but somehow sad.

And after a hundred good-byes

in doorways in a dozen cities,

and kisses I can scarcely recall.

And after films that end long past midnight,

and coming home and seeing, far off,

one lone firefly still searching the dark for its mate,

here you are.

IN A FOREST

Clothed only with dew,

and a cloak of fog so dense I can see my history

in a flickering film cast upon the clouds by lightning:

half-forgotten kisses on

luminous summer afternoons,

a sudden storm when I was five,

when I sat atop a rusty swingset

staring at a tornado tickling the earth

like the finger of a furtive lover,

soaked by rain as warm as blood.

Like the rain that now

taps at my shoulders,

punctuating the recollections of a life –

but for a handful of sad days – almost charmed.

A train of ants navigates

the peninsulas of my toes,

while I ask questions the moon

seems unprepared to answer:

If we follow our dreams, where do they lead us?

Where does the sparkle go when it fades from a lover's eyes?

How much of this moment will I remember?

I linger in the weeds all night,

and near dawn find the answers

in the smell of the breeze rustling through the cool grass,

in the silent fountains of sand kicked into the air by an ant lion,

in the first rumors of light creeping through the trees,

like smiling ghosts on their way to paradise.

Hotel Drama

This is a silence I've heard before:

the rustle of sheets half a sigh away from sleep,

the stuff goodbyes are made of.

What do you say to the people in your dreams?

Am I half man, half monster,

and are you as suspicious of their smiles?

And of your lovers there:

Do you tell them not to touch you?

Do they sit wondering in the half-light

when it was you slipped away?

Is it marked on some sad calendar

the moment when things turned,

the second when your eyes

began to see me differently?

Outside, a train moans its sad moan,

and on the television screen in the hotel lobby,

actors long forgotten play out a drama

that hasn't half the sting of our own.

I would change the channel, if I could.

MAGIC

The show has gone on for years.

I'm tired. My hands shake as I stare into the stage lights.

Audience of children, of the jaded, of whispering dust.

I reach out to pull the swords from the barrel that surrounds you

and find I am bound by chains.

Your tears shine like crystals as they fall to the floor.

Through the water of the tank

you have never looked more beautiful.

As the bubbles from my mouth tickle my eyelids

I pray you are the last sight I see.

In the land of the dead, I hear music

that sounds like the heartbeat of a sick machine.

In the bathrooms the dead sniff the counters,

their howling echoing from behind the row of doors.

I pull the pick from my mouth and unlock the last door,

which opens to reveal another door,

behind which lies still another.

I pull endless veils from the mouths of ghouls,

and amuse wraiths for hours with the same card tricks

they've been seeing for centuries

but forget each time the moon gives way to the sun.

My wand is here in some dark corner,

or underneath a rickety seat.

The crowd surges forward,

hungry for what I cannot give.

Rabbit become rabbit's foot, become rabbit again.

You hold the seer's hand and shake your head,

but you have brought me back from the dead.

I don't know if you can see me,

a ripple in the air as if in some spectral mirror,

but then I see you smile.

I told you I would return one day,

and I stand at the edge of the stage,

shrouded in smoke,

chains at my feet,

shivering, naked, in the winter air,

revealed to be alive by the glimmer in your eyes.

OUR NEIGHBORHOOD

There, off the roads leading to riches and ruin,

these gateways to promise:

simple assemblages of brick,

oaks plucked from tree farms

and brass-plaqued cornices of stone.

Neighborhoods of the legions

washed in on waves of layered silicon

and Internet clothing-catalogue empires.

Homes once filled with earnest families

and children of promise and privilege,

become living rooms littered with discarded cables

where squat spiders guard their corner shrines,

and breakfast nooks, lit by lazy moonlight,

ponder rushed meals that might have been.

By starlight, the people are leaving,

in detailed minivans,

in lumbering SUVs

and sleek, indistinct sedans.

They line the roads to the coastline

they always meant to visit,

linger at the shore,

and board long boats for the center of the ocean,

where waterspouts twitch like animated sprites

lifted from the DVDs of their distracted toddlers

and lightning dances languidly with the warm, sweet rain.

When Mysteries Deepen

This is the time of night when mysteries deepen,

when the going away and the coming home

pass each other like old ghosts,

nothing waving silently at nothing,

and the seconds slipping by shrug at one another and grin,

waiting for what comes next,

which is the change from one dream to another,

heartbreak and listlessness become a meadow lit by strange sunshine.

You swat away your bangs and the stars ripple,

and when you brush your hand over mine

you mask secrets that will take me a lifetime to learn.

Ours is a story I have longed to write,

and I transcribe the words from your whispers,

from the letters you tap against my chest as your fingers twitch in
sleep.

Across town, a train's horn sounds,

and out front: the plaintive cry of a cranky cat.

We smile because we both hear it, and tomorrow we'll hear it still.

LINE OF SIGHT

We see different things in the distance,

and who can say one of us is right

and the other wrong?

Our distance is no different than dreams:

Each is as valid to the dreamer

as incoherent to the lunch listener.

My cadre of white pines

is your gaggle of waterspouts.

And to you my rolling wave of fog

is no more than a bloated cloud,

squatting idly on its haunches.

I would trade my eyes for yours,

so I could see your distance

and know what lies ahead.

Perhaps a half-dozen fewer failures

would make all the difference.

Your Well

I follow your well fathoms deep,

past grubs sleeping in the embrace

of the sweet earth,

past rivers leading to invisible cities,

past the fossilized skeletons

of creatures we cannot imagine,

who centuries ago forgot

more than you and I will ever know.

CARPENTRY

Crying and screaming.

That's what it sounds like.

But you can only tell up close, ear against the front door.

From far away it could be a cat on a windowsill,

an air conditioner on its last legs,

or the whine of a power tool in the hands of a carpenter,

sweating, intent,

certain that when he's done

he'll have built it better than last time.

GOING HOME

Some think too much about leaving,

and some try too hard to stay.

I know the time comes when it comes,

an old friend, resting his hand on your shoulder.

I want to know who will lean over me

that last time,

so I can thank them now —

and also apologize for the moment

when I'll turn away,

when this world washes away,

and the next place fades into view.

Cloudless summer sky and endless prairie,

or a break in the trees that leads

deep into the forest.

The goosebumps when we find the way out,

reaching a shaking hand toward the last door leading to home.

SAMMIE

At the vet,

Sammie, our tiny tiger cat,

Twitches her head left and right

as the vet tech cleans out her ears.

"She's seventeen," I tell her.

"Seventeen? Wow!" the vet tech says.

She smiles,

but her smile quickly fades,

because she knows we'll be back soon enough

for the last time.

At home, Sammie's in my lap.

I've been forgiven.

She falls asleep,

and a few minutes later she is so warm

I think she just might live forever.

LIFE IN THE RAIN

A hundred years have passed

and still it's raining all over the world.

The mountains wash into muddy seas,

and to beaches, long vacant, the people now return,

to look out on steely waters, at the clouds overhead,

always moving, never to disappear,

that bring the rain to this weary world.

Naps grow longer,

and the days are passed in slumber,

dreamers dreaming of their water world where billions of tiny boats

cross and crisscross a planet where the tallest of trees

are playgrounds for fish as large as ocean liners.

The nights are the best times,

the pit pat on the roof of the cabin

become the beating in rapt hearts huddled about a fire

in large rooms where hams hang from rafters,

the pit pat become the metronome

that guides the words of the storyteller,

spinning fantastic tales of a golden desert where it never rains.

The children are astounded,

and they slip off to that bright land,

where carrion birds circle in an empty sky,

where the children lie down in the sand, oh so tired,

waiting for the buzzards to pluck out their eyes,

waiting for the sun to set (although it never does),

waiting for the storm clouds they know are there

if they could only turn their heads to see.

Just as well,

thinks the storyteller,

standing over slumbering children who will, in time,

forget the desert and will walk out into the rain,

only the gray haze in their heads,

never to look back.

THESE TRAILING YEARS

Please don't be like that.

So much promise squandered.

So many arguments won and lost,

only to be forgotten in the haze of morning.

On the last day,

and it will come,

I hope you'll remember that first kiss

in that darkened theater.

Years ago, I left behind

the doe-eyed liars

and fair-haired failers.

Once in a while,

the phone rings late at night.

I no longer answer.

The things we should be thankful for

are scattered at our feet.

Step over them carefully,

and leave them for those

who will be smart enough

to be more grateful.

When I was younger,

every sentence ended with a laugh.

Now it's deadly serious,

here in these trailing years,

all muted laughter and dull barbs,

turning us always in and out of love.

THINGS LOST AND FORGOTTEN

Our lives passed like a careless whisper.

One day, you and I will cease our musings and murmurings,

and death will put us exactly where we need to be.

The office minions and factory workers stand silent

in the last rays of a weary sun.

The ghosts of soldiers wander aimless,

because all the battles have ended.

The specters of our cats and dogs, lost long ago,

wait for us just beyond the veil.

The lightbulb on the hand-me-down lamp

sings and brightens, before – pop! – it goes out forever.

Here in the last moment,

as the stars disappear one by one,

and darkness swallows everything,

I want to say something meaningful.

Order comes at the end.

All the things I couldn't remember

now come to me in a flood,

and all the things I'd lost

are in a dusty pile in the living room.

Lifetime after listless lifetime,

you were always on my mind.

THE MAGICIANS OF THIS AGE

Once we were waiting to be born.

But that was a lifetime ago.

If I had an ancient torch,

I would gladly pass it to you,

if only to be relieved of the burden.

Of these countless acts,

how many will matter?

It was always you.

Tell me the secrets of your heart,

and I will tell you mine,

and we will be the magicians of this age.

Or words to that effect.

In dreams,

so many lovers and villains,

stern teachers and sleepy librarians,

tongue-tied orators and shadowy houseguests,

failed warriors and disappointed ghosts.

They all had your face.

142

I'll See It Again

I look for you in the windows of the town,

in every passing car,

in the clouds crossing in front of the moon,

in scattered dreams that, upon waking, are quickly forgotten.

Someone once told me:

"Do not travel to meet the moving glacier.

It will come to you."

Me? I've gone as far as I can.

You know the way from here.

The look in your eyes that I've seen before,

I'll see it again.

And I am sorry.

For what, I'm sure I don't know.

TELL ME HOW YOU ARE

These days run long.

I hear voices that aren't there, always asking.

Sometimes I wish it was just you and me,

sitting in a corner bar,

or on a park bench crusted with peeling paint.

I know we've fallen short,

but I don't care, and as we sit in the half-light

that hides all that's best hidden,

you could tell me how you are.

Some dreams still live.

Like moth wings fluttering against the damp earth,

they're not nearly as fragile as they might seem.

We could talk as the cars thin out

on the broken avenues.

And you don't even have to speak.

Just keep looking at me as the moment passes,

And all the moments that come after.

www.ingramcontent.com/pod-product-compliance
Lightning Source LLC
Chambersburg PA
CBHW031414120626
46545CB00006B/2136